S0-ABI-608

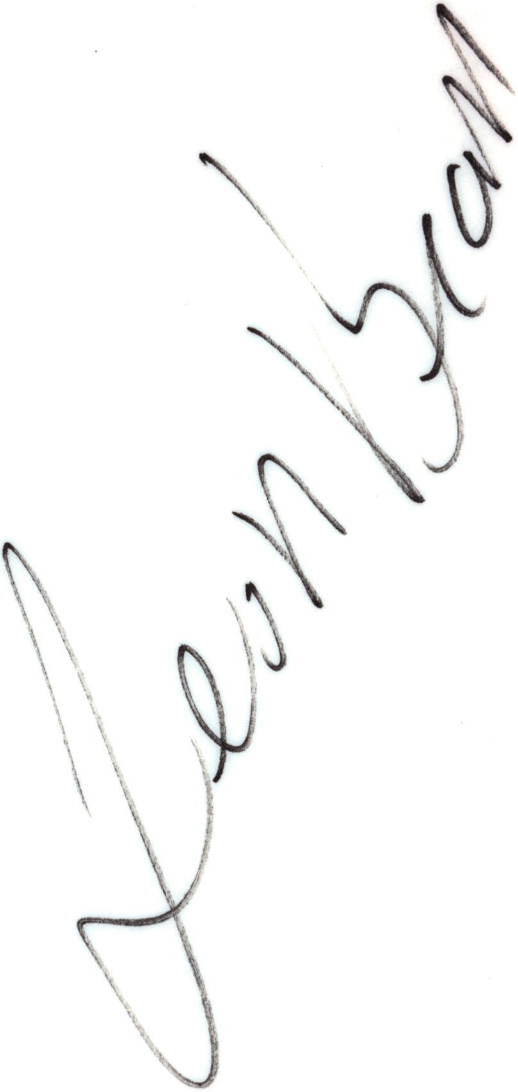

# EARNING MY WINGS

By

Leon Franklin Bean III

*AuthorHouse™*
*1663 Liberty Drive, Suite 200*
*Bloomington, IN 47403*
*www.authorhouse.com*
*Phone: 1-800-839-8640*

*AuthorHouse™ UK Ltd.*
*500 Avebury Boulevard*
*Central Milton Keynes, MK9 2BE*
*www.authorhouse.co.uk*
*Phone: 08001974150*

*© 2001, 2003, 2006 Leon F. Bean III. All rights reserved.*

*No part of this book may be reproduced, stored in a retrieval system, or transmitted by any means without the written permission of the author.*

*First published by AuthorHouse 8/21/2006*

*ISBN: 0-7596-3156-5 (e)*
*ISBN: 0-7596-3157-3 (sc)*

*Printed in the United States of America*
*Bloomington, Indiana*

*This book is printed on acid-free paper.*

# ACKNOWLEDGMENTS

My greatest appreciation and love goes to my beautiful mother for encouraging me to write from the heart and to follow my dreams.

You guided me through school and opened my eyes when I could not see. You always had that certain spark and appeal that could always soothe the savage beast. That in itself makes you an amazing entertainer. Yes, you truly are an amazing entertainer.

It seems just like yesterday, when I wiped away the tears from my eyes and looked into your eyes for the last time. I was in white and you soon would be too.

If dancing is said to be the root of our heritage of people who struggle to overcome boundaries a dream that's never ending in remembering you, keeps the dream alive. I learned that loving myself is the first step toward loving others.

Respecting your elders shows that you have respect for yourself. Your smile and your song will live in me til I live no more. You were a gracious host in all that you did for me and others. It was your warm smile that touched the hearts of many and your gentle spirit will now endure in all of them as they remember you with a smile of their own.

Remembering that through Christ all things are possible.

This book represents the culmination of a healing process. I would like to thank my step-father for having the patience to deal with me and my old, rickety chair making noise while I typed, non-stop through the wee hours of the night. This was not done intentionally, but often between 1:00 a.m. to 2:00 a.m., my writers block would fade into the darkness and the light of inspiration would emerge. Many, many times, I thought I would not finish, but thanks to my childhood friend, Lamont Hogan, I persevered. After what seemed like thousands of calls, he always provided a listening ear and words of encouragement.

# CONTENTS

Introduction ............................................................. 1

Remembrance: Early Days ..................................... 7

Letters of Appreciation: A Teacher's Reward ..................... 19

Diary Page: Michael & Me ................................. 45

Letter of Forgiveness: All The Things We Didn't Say ........... 63

Letter of Remembrance: Missing You Trisha ..................... 75

Diary Page: Misled By Lust ............................... 123

Diary Page: Sugar Candy and Mints ................................. 149

Remembrance: Your Calling ............................................. 163

Resolutions: Inner Peace ..................................... 219

ABOUT THE AUTHOR ..................................... 231

## **Introduction**

My how times have changed from what they used to be. Looking back through this old photo album at pictures of myself, I have noticed how Little Leon has changed over the years. I have taken just these two pictures out to view – just these two. There is one of me as a child – a little one at four months old. The other is me at age 26. Wow, look at the difference. When I look into Leon's eyes, I see a mighty change has overtaken him. That free unbounded spirit and those big round, brown eyes were once the epitome of innocence. The peace that once surrounded Leon's face now shows the hard realities of the world – the truth of a Black Man's Truth – in a world that lacks complete understanding of self identification. I see slavery in big Leon. His eyes tell me so very much. The reflection of Lee has the ability to take over your mind and your body and your soul. His eyes hold so much pain that I can barely stand to look into them. But I have to look into his eyes to see the truth. And sometimes, that's more than I can handle.

*Letters of Appreciation*

*Earning My Wings*

Leon is still carrying chains around his neck. I call it new world slavery – chains around your mind, rather than your neck. He has become sick to the evils of the world system. I see prejudice in his eyes. I see a constant battle. Leon has been made by the world. He has conformed to the world's trends to fit in, but true happiness for Leon is like a tee shirt – it only comes down half way. I look closer at those eyes. I see a man who is struggling to be at peace in so many ways. There are so many forms of peace – peace of mind, body and soul. The lust factor is heavy in him. He often welcomes lust because love takes too long or it hurts too much. Lust may not be as complicated as love and it may not require as much work – but it never fills the void.

My God, look at those eyes. Where does a guy get eyes like that? They are so beautiful, but they are dim now. The luster, that glow – where has it gone? Once upon a time, I could see Jesus in your eyes. When you were a baby, did that old devil come in and corrupt your soul? Did he tell you that you were worthless? I know what he did. He stole from you the very thing

*Letters of Appreciation*

*Earning My Wings*

you loved the most – your family and your youth. I have watched you shape yourself into a strong man who has overcome so many obstacles. In retrospect, they might not seem like much, but they are specific to you for your growth. You have walked into situations that you really should not have walked out of, but by the grace of God, you are still standing. Your faith has been unwavering and your loyalty to the everlasting has kept you strong throughout bad relationships and good ones – throughout sickness and health. You, Leon Franklin Bean, III are a true testimony. A man must ultimately know himself. He must be the master of his universe. Knowing yourself better than any one person will alleviate any false ideas that may be placed on you or around you. Be true and forthcoming in your approaches. You were planted in this life to always continue to grow and open doors to teach others to grow and to be honest with themselves and not live to follow the world's system because it will fail you every time.

*Letters of Appreciation*

## Remembrance: Early Days

What do I remember most about our 4$^{th}$ floor apartment on Linden Avenue? Rats, mice and cock roaches. We used broken bottles to plug the holes inside the apartment to keep the rats and mice out. A few mice still managed to slip through the cracks in the floors, but nothing kept the roaches from moving in. It didn't matter how many me and my mother stepped on – they just kept multiplying. Now I'm not a fan of roaches, but as an only child, I got bored quickly. I needed something to do so I would sit on the floor and trap the roaches and play with them as if they were my friends. Truthfully, those roaches became my best friends. It was how I filled my lonely days.

I lived with my mother in that apartment from ages 2 through 8. I learned how to wash dishes by standing on a stool, fix TV dinners and wash sheets. Usually, the TV dinners wound up on my sheets during the night. If it wasn't the TV dinner it was those extra glasses of water that I snuck from the jug in the refrigerator. I hated telling my mom about my accidents. I already felt miserable about waking up in either vomit or piss, but to add insult to injury, she would make me get up and wash my sheets in detergent that always made my skin itch. I stopped

*Letters of Appreciation*

*Earning My Wings*

eating TV dinners and I stopped sneaking water from the jug in the refrigerator.

My mother went to church every Sunday. I didn't have a choice. I was always fidgeting. Mom was always telling me to be still, but I couldn't keep still on those hard pews at St. John's Baptist Church. The pews didn't have cushions, and I didn't have much of a butt to begin with, and what I had went numb from sitting for so long. Sometimes I would catch my mother drawing in church. She drew flowers and figures on blank paper or the back of the church program. She was no Picasso, but she did alright. I called it fidget art. My mother had many faces depending on her mood. If she was displeased, she would break down her face, squint her eyes and tighten her lips. She, like most mothers thought that if I was fidgeting, I wasn't paying attention to the pastor's sermon. But I was. After we got home from church I would do my rendition of the pastor. I knew better than to pull that in church. That would have caused some major problems...like a slap in the mouth. I pulled that trick one time and got embarrassed in front of the whole congregation when my mother slapped the taste out of my mouth. I was trying to hold back the tears, so I looked at the pictures of Jesus. I think he was embarrassed for me too. I was always mocking the

*Letters of Appreciation*

*Earning My Wings*

pastor, or somebody else. I guess that's why they started calling me Lil' Leon. I wanted to be in the spotlight, but for some reason, I always seemed to be running from it.

After Sunday service I looked forward to hanging out with my best friend Tyrone. We would run up and down the alley, ride our bikes and do things that most boys do. Tyrone and I were cool. As a matter of fact, we were like brothers. Even if he was punished, I could always go inside his house and chill. It beat playing outside by myself or back at our apartment with the roaches. There were so many times when I wished that I had siblings. It wouldn't have mattered if they were younger or older. I just wanted someone who could watch over me, or who was close in age. I wanted someone to talk to and play with. I was an only child and a lonely child. Because of my loneliness, I began creating imaginary friends. My favorite past time was living in a fictitious world with my newly invented friends. My mother noticed how lonely I was and decided to get me lots of pets. We had a cat named Kitty who had sixteen cats. Three out of the sixteen kittens died and the rest had to be sent to the pound. We kept one kitten and I called him Skeet. I really didn't want my mother to send the other kittens away, but we couldn't feed them all. We buried the three that died right

*Letters of Appreciation*

*Earning My Wings*

away in the backyard before Kitty could get to them. God only knows what she would have done to them. I had little funerals for them. My new friend Skeet would be the kitten, turned adult cat that would leave a lasting impression on me. He was my super hero and my brother. My other pets were tad poles, two hamsters named Peter and Timberly, four lizards, goldfish and a dog named Princess. Now Princess was my baby girl. She was fat as a butter ball and always wanted to be hugged and kissed. I loved her so much, but I think she loved me more. My pets were my friends and my family. They were my brothers, sisters and cousins too. But I was still lonely.

I started singing to free my mind and stretch my voice. Even as a child, I had a high pitched voice. To be quite honest, I sounded like Michael Jackson of the Jackson 5. When I was in the $1^{st}$ and $2^{nd}$ grade, I couldn't wait to get home from school so that I could stand in the lobby of the building on the first floor and sing up a storm. I would make up songs to sing. I loved to here my voice echo, but most of all, I loved singing because I felt like the whole world was there cheering me on. I would look at the black and white tiled floor and imagine that they were people watching me and cheering for me as I sang. It made me feel so good to be loved by so many people, yet in the back of my mind

*Letters of Appreciation*

*Earning My Wings*

I still had to remember that it was only a figment of my imagination. But every day I'd do a command performance in the lobby until my mother came home. What a difference it would have made in my life if we had music by the Jackson 5, or if there were other kids singing in the house with me. Maybe I would not have been so shy. Not much has changed about my shyness. I often wish that someone would have paid attention to my singing and recognized my talent. Even then I felt like a piece of clay waiting to be molded. I just needed somebody who believed in me and it seemed like it was taking forever for that person to come along. Still, I kept on dreaming.

Mr. Booker lived up the hall in apartment #1 in our building. He always had rainbow bubble gum in his pocket for me. If I wanted my own pack it would have cost me five cents. Mr. Booker never said much. He always wore a hat and matching full length coat. His outfits made me laugh. It reminded me of our sofa. It broke my heart when Mr. Booker moved out of the building. I could count on him for rainbow bubble gum. When he was around, I wasn't lonely.

When someone asks me about my childhood, I must honestly say that I had good and bad memories. I guess you could say I was pretty much like all the other children, but I knew early on in my life that I

*Letters of Appreciation*

was unique. I often felt like I was here before my time. It was unusual for a child my age to know and understand the power of prayer. But I did. Somehow, I always knew that no matter how difficult life seemed to be, it would eventually come together. Even when I got into trouble – which was a lot I knew things would work out for me. I stayed in trouble. I was always getting my ass whipped. If I didn't know Jesus before, I sure got to know him during those beatings. And he got to know me because I surely called his name.

I often think back to the people I've met along the way. I look at how they have affected my life. Some good and others, not so good. When I talk to people who knew me during these pivotal times in my life, they always say that I had a gentle spirit and that I was a good friend. No one could ever deny that I was a good friend. They thought I was graceful, kindhearted with a gentle spirit – and I was – but I also had a dark side. My soul was trapped in that dark world. Sure, I stayed to myself, and truthfully, I was happy when I was alone, but alone was the worst thing for me to be.

*Letters of Appreciation*

# Letters of Appreciation: A Teacher's Reward

I asked a teacher of my early years in school this question; "What could I give you to tell you thanks for all you have done for me and given me, over the years?" She said, "stay in school and learn to give back when you are called on. Never forget how important it is to educate yourself and others and over the years that I have known you, you have done just that in more ways than one. That in itself is reward enough for me."

When I think about my early years in school, certain teachers come to mind such as Mrs. Clayton. Everyone knew her and would tease her for the way she looked. They were so mean to her, they would even shoot spitballs at her. Now, as I think about those things that happened in the past, I knew they weren't right but I did not speak up. Why? Why didn't I speak up for the right thing? Maybe because I knew the other kids would start picking on me. I knew I did not want that, especially being called the teacher's pet. That was a

*Letters of Appreciation*

*Earning My Wings*

no, no. Kids sometimes make things more than what they are. Mrs. Clayton did not look like a witch of any kind, nor was she a bad person, it was her voice, that I will never forget. In spite of all of that she was a nice woman and teacher.

About 18 years later, I saw Mrs. Clayton. She really didn't remember me until I started talking to her. She made me feel so good. I told her how well I was doing and she told me to keep keeping on. When I saw her smile, it was like music to my ears.

I haven't been back to my old grammar school in years. Occasionally, I'll ride pass and remember how much I loved to play on that playground. So many things in my life had changed from the days when I use to run up, down and all around the wood chips of Mt. Royal School #66. When I think about School #66, one other special woman comes to mind, Mrs. Sachs, the librarian. She would read to us like we were her own children. The whole class would sit together on the floor and Mrs. Sachs would read stories to us. It was so exciting to hear her read. I always loved her because she was so professional and

*Letters of Appreciation*

*Earning My Wings*

special. She had such a beautiful smile and the most beautiful white hair that she could give Santa Claus a run for his money. I dream of reading to my children with the same tender loving care that you read to us. All my thanks and heart felt appreciation goes out to Mrs. Sachs.

One could never forget a teacher as noble and as unforgettable as the one and only Mrs. Scott. They don't make them like her anymore. I was in the second grade, just learning how to write in script, and not all that well mind you. I don't remember much about Mrs. Scott except that she loved to keep me after school. She couldn't get enough of calling me "Mr. Bean." "Mr. Bean, is that you talking over there?" I would say, "No." After being called two or three times for the same thing, she knew it was me. Talking and all, I still send all my love to you! It was a joy to go to your class.

I was about seven or eight years old and the school disciplinarian was Mr. Randolf Robinson, a name I could never forget. He was always lurking around some unsuspecting

*Letters of Appreciation*

*Earning My Wings*

corner, waiting for trouble, so he could rectify it with some disciplinary action. The most popular of these actions was removal from school. I knew whenever a teacher said go to Mr. Robinson, your stomach turned and your head would spin. I remember all too well being sent to his office on many occasions. He always had this look about him, not playful, but very serious. You couldn't get over on him, not even if you tried. He was not for the playing or talking out of line or out and out disrespecting that the other kids gave the teachers. He was NOT HAVING IT! Do you remember that old expression, "Barking up the wrong tree!" He was the one tree you didn't want to bark up against.

I remember him laying back in his swivel chair, which always seemed to have a squeaky sound like it needed to be oiled. He would look directly at you and say, "Have a seat!" He always kept piles of work books for you to do. Mr. Robinson also had a nice side to him as well. I was lucky in that I got to see that side as well. He would let the kids from all over the

*Letters of Appreciation*

*Earning My Wings*

school come to his class and paint ceramic animals, Indian heads,dogs, and other things of that sort. He was always the one to schedule skating trips to the famous *Shake and Bake* recreation center, but only the kids with good performance would be allowed to go. When I think about how good those days were and all the fun we had it makes me miss those days. However, those days had their time and place and they were well taken advantage of for all they were worth. Mr. Robinson, you showed me that negative behavior has consequences and good behavior has rewards. Thank you for showing me guidance at the beginning and at the end of my early school years. A job well done.

Mrs. Briscoe, I'll never forget you and what you did for me and what you continually do for me. You introduced me to the Arts and you kept on me with a passion about the importance of writing, performing, staging and timing dramatics. You always had faith in me and for that I am most thankful. At such a young age it meant a lot. All the time you invested did not go

*Letters of Appreciation*

*Earning My Wings*

unnoticed, it helped to build my self esteem. I was in the third grade when I was first introduced to Mrs. Briscoe. When I was told she was a special education teacher, I did not know how to respond. What were they saying? Was I not bright enough to be with the other kids? I knew there was some kind of mistake. When recess came, my old class mates were passing me in the hallway. I did not see them as much as I had before. At first it bothered me but as time went on I got over it. The kids in the other classes would call the kids in my class DEC kids and say we were stupid. I only accepted the comments made that we had special needs. By the teachers attending to these needs, we could be better students and could keep up with the fast pace of the kids in other classes. Mrs. Briscoe never made us feel less than any of the other kids. As time went on, it became less important for me to worry about class titles. That nonsense did not effect me in the least. I remember Mrs. Briscoe encouraging me to do my famous puppet show. I loved to make the character's come alive and I loved to captivate the class'

*Letters of Appreciation*

attention. Mrs. Briscoe would always be in charge of assemblies and special programs, especially arranging dance routines. The program that put me on the map was the famous "Praying Mantis." Playing the role of the praying mantis, I would attack the prey. I got to drag a fellow classmate across the stage. The response that I got from the crowd was incredible. Everyone loved it.

I must admit my behavior in class was not always peaches and cream, I assure you. I wasn't always an angel. On many occasions, I would give Mrs. Briscoe a run for her money and drive her up the wall. I guess I thought I could get away with anything but she was not having that from a little kid. She would grab me by my arm and march me down the hall to the office without hesitation. She would then say the one thing I drastically did not want to hear, "I am going to call your mother!" I definitely did not want that because my mother would say in a very nice but threatening way, "I am going to have

*Letters of Appreciation*

something for you when you get home." I knew what that meant; my goose was cooked.

Things weren't always that rocky after my attitude adjustments and I settled down. But if I got out of line, Mrs. Briscoe didn't think twice about telling me that she would call my mother. One of her most famous threats was when she called me by my first, middle, and last name, Leon Franklin Bean, do you want me to call your mother?" She would say it in such a voicerous way.

Mrs. Briscoe always stayed in my corner. She was my Lena Horne through stormy weather. She was there through sunshine and rain. When I was low and in a distant, non-talkative mood, she would come to me and ask me what the problem was. I did not want to say because my mother would always say not to talk about the things that happen in the home. Keep those things to yourself, she advised. It was hard for me to do, however, because I did not know why things were happening the way they

*Letters of Appreciation*

*Earning My Wings*

were. Mrs. Briscoe would always make me feel safe and comfortable and tell me everything was going to be okay!

Who could forget Mrs. O'Neill my second grade teacher. She was a class act. She would always treat us so nice; not like a meanie. When our class would take special tests, she would give us *M&Ms* candy and then would do something totally unexpected. Mrs. O'Neill would put on a *Barry Manilow* record or other hot group of the 1980s like *Police* and *Men at Work* and the class would go wild. We would get up and sing and stretch. We had so much fun in her class. Thanks for making second grade a grade to remember.

Mrs. Wright, the cafeteria supervisor, was not to be played with. She could be evil as a whip and smart as a tack but she never really bothered me because I never had to wait in line to get a free lunch. If I was in line to buy something, it would be only for an ice cream sandwich and butterscotch cookies. I would buy them like they were going out of style. Mrs. Wright always had a mothering way about her. She treated all of us like

*Letters of Appreciation*

*Earning My Wings*

we were her children. She would always do extra special things like bringing movies to school so students that were good could see them. But never in my wildest dreams did I think she would have the tape of all tapes. The first copy of the Michael Jackson's *Thriller* tape on the making of the video. I had never seen the video until then. That's why it was so extra special. All the other kids would gather in the multi-purpose center and watch the horror in amazement. We love you, Mrs. Wright. You definitely made being a student at Mt. Royal School #66, a place where any kid that comes in your path receive the royal treatment. You made lunch time more than just a break from class. It was like coming home to a hug from warm loving arms.

Another person that has been on my mind was a cleaning lady at the school. She would always speak to the students. Sometimes I would see her in the cafeteria and I would recognize her by the old dark gray dress she wore. She was a small lady about five feet tall and had a gentle spirit about her. So it just seemed okay for me to ask her if I could borrow a

*Letters of Appreciation*

*Earning My Wings*

quarter so that I could buy milk. I usually would have the money but on this occasion, I did not. She gave me the money and I told her I would repay her. The next morning, I was looking for her and could not find her. I had the money to repay her but she was no where to be found. When I found out that she had passed away, I was in disbelief. How could someone so nice be gone? When they were taking a collection for her I held onto the money because I still could not believe that the same lady that I was talking to the day before was gone. I prayed to God and asked him to tell her that I had her money and wanted her to know it. I was waiting for her and I wanted to tell her thank you.

The French call them them "creme a la crème;" these teachers that were nothing less than the best. I learned the most valuable lessons about myself, what I was capable of and what I had to do to achieve bigger and better things. Being taught about one's history and ancestry is essential to one's growth. You have both taught me that respect for one's self should come along with respecting others. With those components, success is

*Letters of Appreciation*

*Earning My Wings*

inevitable. Its all in the way you rate success and achievements in your day to day living, knowing there's always something to learn. These are things that I learned from Miss P. Thomas and Mrs. S. Nickles.

When I entered into the eighth grade, the one thing that I looked forward to was being in a class with the great Mrs. Fuller. She was always the talk of the school among the students and faculty. It was always Mrs. Fuller this and Mrs. Fuller that. When I was in elemetary school, I would always go to programs and would love to hear Mrs. Fuller play the piano. It always made me think about my favorite Aunt who played piano and sang gospel music in church. Remembering the way she graced our ears with the subtle way she played that piano. She always set my ears on fire. She played that piano! Trust me, she did! She was a bird soaring across the sky with the Lord guiding her wings. It is so hard to say all the things that I feel for you Mrs. Fuller, but I will just sum it up and say my hat's off to you for all

*Letters of Appreciation*

that you have done for me and the entire school system. BRAVO, BRAVO, take a bow! You so desire it!

*Letters of Appreciation*

## Diary Page: Michael & Me

People always ask me what do I think about Michael Jackson's song, "Man in the Mirror." Whenever I hear the question, it takes me back to Christmas time in 1983, the best time of the year for children around the world. I was nine years old and I remember being in the back of the classroom listening to all of my favorite Christmas carols, like *Frosty*, *Rudolf the Red Nose Reindeer*, and other classics. I saw a Jackson Five record laying next to some other records and since I had never heard of the group before, I thought I would take a listen to it. When I played the record, I was immediately taken back. There was such harmony in their voices that it sent shivers through me. The way they projected the range of their voices really impressed me.

It was Michael's voice, in particular, that stood out from the rest. I continued to listen to the music in the back of the class and started to hum and sing along with the record. Their music

*Diary Page*

*Earning My Wings*

made me want to sing, but I was too shy to sing in front of people, so I just kept my little voice to myself. Then the kids in the class said, "Leon, is that you singing?" I didn't know if they thought my singing was good or bad and I did not want to find out. I was so shy, even if they liked it, I still would not sing for them, so I said, "NO! It's not me it's the record." I hurried away from the back of the class so my classmates would not start picking on me again. They would always tease me about the way I looked and dressed and especially about my glasses. "Hey everybody, four eyes is trying to sing," one of them shouted. Everyone began to laugh. When I came home from school that day, I had forgotten all about their laughter and I couldn't wait to tell my mother about hearing this group called the Jackson Five.

Christmas Day finally arrived and I could not wait to see what Santa had left under the tree for me. Mom would not let me open all my gifts; I had to wait until we came back from visiting other family members. We went to my step-father's mother house and after a day of being hugged, kissed, and

*Diary Page*

*Earning My Wings*

squeezed, I was ready to go home and finish opening my gifts. Almost all of the gifts seemed to be something to wear except for a real thin package. I don't want it, I thought to myself, but opened it anyway. I could not believe my eyes. It was the Jackson Five Christmas record! I hugged Mom for making my Christmas the happiest day of my life. I could now play the record all day, every day and sing along. Soon, it was the middle of summer and still I was singing about mommy kissing Santa Claus.

Six years later, I finally got a chance to see Michael live in concert. I won two tickets from a radio show for the opening night in Washington, DC. My Grandfather took me down to the radio station to pick up the tickets. I then had to decide who to take with me, my Mom or my girlfriend. I wanted them both to go but that was impossible, so I took my Mom. That night, October 13, 1989, I finally got a chance to hear and see Mr. Magic for myself with the woman I love the most.

*Diary Page*

*Earning My Wings*

The first time I saw him left a lasting impression of energy personified. Courage, devotion, concentration, enthusiasm entrapped by perfection were all words that came to mind. He looks at himself as a pure instrument of nature, vocally and physically. He emotionally overwhelms you at the mere sight of him. His grace is uncanny, his poise as still as the summer night. Michael J. Jackson, this man has been a driving force in my life for the past 14 years. He is unlike any individual I have seen. He has helped me grow as an individual. There was a time in my life when I did not know who I was or what I wanted to be. I was ethnically lost, insecure, unaware of society's impression of me and what my impression of myself should be. Some of these impressions of what I should be as a man, I learned at home but something I did not learn growing up at home were certain things that were not a topic for conversation over the dinner table. I was unaware that masculinity and femininity could be shared in so many ways. The slightest thing you do that is not

*Diary Page*

*Earning My Wings*

masculine, quote unquote, you are automatically labeled, stereotyped as this or that. There is no in between when you could very well be very masculine and have some slightly feminine ways. Who is the judge? Society of course, they are the ones who make things more then what they are. It is sad because what you feel inside your heart strongly should over come all the rhetoric.

I have heard people say the sky is the limit; reach for your goals, strive, dream and all the things you dream will come true. Sounds so simple and it is, but why is it that so many of us don't see our lives as a success in a stereotypical society that rates success on material wealth rather than paying more attention on how we want to live. The major needs of the world, like simple respect for our fellow man, have gone out the door along with respect for ourselves. Helping our fellow man or woman without our hand out for compensation is a rarity. It hurts me to my heart. I am so concerned about the children of the world that we live in today. There is not that much compassion shown for

*Diary Page*

*Earning My Wings*

our brothers and sisters in the places where you would expect it to be. The concept that people get in their heads is that as long as it is not infringing on their life, they shouldn't be bothered.

To applaud the cheat, the sham artist only adds to the problem of cheating the system. Is that anyway to show success? No, I don't think so. It is so important for you to have self worth and morals. These are the things that will haul you over in the long run. So that is why you need to show the right examples for your children because they watch you and learn the good along with the bad. Remember, no one is perfect, so for once in your life give it a shot because you only have one life to live. I have learned so much about myself since I have been performing. Self expression, the art of one's ability to transform oneself is so amazing.

I feel that God has given us the bodies he wants us to have. Of course, he has created us in a certain form and fashion. He also gives us the choice to venture out to recreate ourselves and our surroundings. We are not limited to where we choose to live

*Diary Page*

as far as what town, city, state or country. God has given us a choice. Choice is the key word. He has also given us the unique ability to take advantage of plastic cosmetic enhancement; something that now is more mainstream than ever before. If there is something about yourself that you want to change you have the preference to change it or not. If you don't like it change it, especially if you have to resources to take advantage of them whatever they maybe. I relate some of these characteristics to myself and Michael Jackson mainly because he displays his creative abilities through his visual appearance as well as his artistic performances. It is just riveting as if he were sliding up and down the stage with ease.

I have always wanted to have attention drawn to me, good attention that is, without a lot of negative vibes and foolish innuendoes that seem to come along with any kind of success or popular acclaim. The power and control of his facial expressions, the slightest movement can send you into shear astonishment at the grace. I had been studying Mr. Jackson for

*Diary Page*

*Earning My Wings*

quite some time and I found out what it was that made him the mystery he was to all of us. He told us time and time again, but we thought it was just a lot of gibberish. Michael, like me, is alarmingly shy and sensitive.

Through the 1990s society tried to run his name through the mud, as recklessly as little kids in a classroom. They wanted to know personal things about his life; not because they were truly concerned about justice. When you are looking for the truth, you don't do the things that they did. My, how the world has changed when searching for the truth equates to dehumanizing individuals. Defaming them hurts more than you know. It hurts the fans because if it were a teacher you had from an early age, how would it feel to have them dragged through the dirt. There is a right way to do business and a wrong way. I feel in my heart of hearts, Michael was done a terrible injustice that hurt him in more ways than could be ever written on paper. No matter, I personally think they went too far and still they did not have

*Diary Page*

*Earning My Wings*

enough. It goes to show you how far people will go to bring you down.

No matter what, I was lucky to have been one of the many impersonators to be gifted with the unique ability to portray Mike, at a time when I was rich with pure heartfelt emotions that only a true impersonator could have. Michael, unlike some, can demand your attention. You had to pay close attention because you did not want to miss anything. His presence wooed us. We did not know why but at the moment it did not matter because it was Michael Jackson. Instead of ignoring him, you wanted to understand him. I think there's a piece of Mr. Jackson in all of us. Thank you Joseph and Katherine Jackson.

*Diary Page*

## Letter of Forgiveness: All The Things We Didn't Say

As I look back on my twenty odd years of my life, many things come to mind but mostly regrets. One of not having the willpower to standup for myself and control my manhood, human manhood that is. It never ceases to amaze me how all the things you've wished will in some way present themselves to you. Unknowingly, you push them aside waiting for what is truly not meant for you; that is unattainable. For you time has passed, but now this is one of those rare occasions when you have one more chance to express all the things we didn't say.

I never knew that I would miss you as much as I do, and I never knew how much of myself I lost when I lost you. You were the grape on the vine who produced the finest wine in the vineyard. How sweet it was to know a true legend such as you, my Grandfather. It seems just like yesterday when you were holding me in your arms cradling me with that look of pride in

*Letter of Forgiveness*

*Earning My Wings*

your eye. I knew deep down inside of you that there was much pain. How could a man hold so much in for so long and how could a man turn his back on his family in more ways than one. I have always learned that there is more to being a father than just being a provider. Anyone can say what I have done for you or I gave you this and that, but grandfather don't you worry I don't blame you because you are only an example of the way you were raised. It is not for me to say if it is right or wrong, only that we all should learn from our mistakes and the mistakes of others. But giving of yourself and your time and love means so very much.

Grandfather, you had so much love to give to your whole family. A heart as good as peach cobbler on a Sunday afternoon. You were a diamond in the rough! You had come so far yet still standing in the same place, not wanting to move because death would follow and destroy you. It would not be where you raised your children or where your father died, or where your mother

*Letter of Forgiveness*

*Earning My Wings*

layed her head, it would be elsewhere and there would be no coming back once you left. The Gate Keeper had his eye on you and he watched everything, read everyone's thoughts, ideas, plans. He gave signals; opportunities for change, but they were left unanswered. So then he stepped in to answer the call and prayers of his faithful servant. He who had cried for so long but he himself was also left unanswered, overlooked and disrespected. The father had seen enough. I don't blame anyone grandfather. There is no need to point fingers anymore, the only person worth fighting for is now gone. So there is only the memory, the image of a time never to return but a love hovering over like the cloud above. When I think about all the things we didn't say, I like to say thank you for stepping in on my life when I needed someone to listen, someone to love, someone to care, someone to be my Grandpop. For when I needed a friend or shelter from the cold or food to eat, you were always there.

You told me of times long ago and battles fought and won. Times of despair and times of joy. In my book, you were always the best. I know I might not have done all the things that were

*Letter of Forgiveness*

*Earning My Wings*

most pleasing to you, but I am sorry. If I could turn back the hands of time, you know I would. You never really spoke much but when you did you were heard loud and clear. I always wondered why you never said I love you or all the sentimental things grandparents say to grandchildren. But in your own way and in your own time, you did say those things.

When I turned sixteen, I had to get those black suede, steel-toe, silvertip cowboy boots with the spurs. It was a dream for me and I asked my grandpop if he could get them for me. Without hesitation he did. I was so happy I could do cartwheels. I even skipped in those boots. No one really knew how much they really meant to me. It was the fact that I asked my Pop, not knowing what his answer would be, I took a chance in asking him. I had never gotten a birthday card or gift from him before, not that it mattered. But 16 years old was it, and he made it a sweet 16!

I proudly wore the boots to school in the ghetto and in my all black high school in Baltimore. They were truly not ready for

*Letter of Forgiveness*

*Earning My Wings*

those boots and little me inside of them. I walked to school trying to avoid anyone seeing me. When I got there and walked into class, the other kids laughed and pointed at me. Laughing all the while, I tried to keep my composure and not cry. So I proudly laughed with them, knowing I loved my boots and I would not take them off. I would, in fact, wear them and nobody or nothing would stop me because I loved them so.

My Pop always had some kind of war story to tell. Proud of his involvement in World War II and his picture in a national world book, he always reminded me of his war days. I would never want to forget, 92nd Division, Buffalo Division, Staff Sergeant. I remember getting thrown out of school and my Grandfather came to the school to get me back in. He started telling the Principal about his involvement in the war. I don't know how we got to that subject but I knew the Principal would have no choice other than letting me back in school just so Pop would stop talking. I was laughing in my head, if only you could hear me laughing. Listen, I always looked at you grandfather as

*Letter of Forgiveness*

*Earning My Wings*

a strong powerful man. With one look he could turn you to stone. I mean you would freeze right in your tracks but you only got that look if you upset him.

It really bothered me when he became ill. I had never known any kind of weakness, illness, pain associated with my Grandfather. I had never seen him cry before, but my mother told me he had cried because he wanted her to do the right thing by me. He did not want me to hurt in any way because of how special I was to him. Pop never talked too much about feelings but he had them and to know him was to love him.

From your dearest and most faithful grandson Leon F. Bean, III; more fondly known as Curly, a nickname my Grandad gave me as a young babe because when I was born I had no hair.

*Letter of Forgiveness*

## Letter of Remembrance: Missing You Trisha

It was the year 1989 and I was in the tenth grade. I was so lonely at high school, far away from everyone and everything that I had once held so close in grammar school. Getting use to a new school and new friends, I just didn't think this high school thing was for me. It wasn't all they said it would be. I had to start all over again and, man, there was too much work involved for me. I wasn't impressed; not at all. They said it would be a place I would never forget; that all my memorable moments would come from this place. I don't think so, not this place. I could not see it, at least not yet.

Then in my sophomore year things began to change. Beyond popular belief, that year, I won tickets to a Michael Jackson concert over the radio. Do you know how big a star he is? He's like so BIG; I can't compare him to anyone now that BIG. WOW! Now, this high school thing was starting to look pretty good. There were so many wonderful things that lay in

*Letter of Remebrance*

*Earning My Wings*

store for me at this legendary high school, Forest Park Senior High School, #406. It was truly more than just a high school, it was a community of sorts. The staff were nurturing and encouraging. Preparing you for the world ahead was their job and for me it meant taking advantage of the opportunities presented. The one thing that I had held so dear was our class motto, "There Is Nothing We Can't Do ... Cause We're the Class of 92!"

I was a shy, little guy in the tenth grade. I didn't have many friends and was what you might call a loner. People said I was an introvert because I stayed to myself and I liked it that way. I seemed always to attract lots of females for friends. I had a few guys as associates but I really did not bother with them much. They tried to give this macho-ego, tough guy approach to everything. Most of them were far from tough. I had no room for it and I think all the girls that called me their friend could tell I wasn't trying to get with that ego maniac, trend follower mess. I considered myself more of a leader than a follower. The

*Letter of Remebrance*

*Earning My Wings*

clothes I wore, no one else in the school would wear because they were too worried about everyone's opinion. Their opinions didn't matter to me since I did not come to school to be the best dressed and win a trophy. I came to do what I had to do then leave. I wasn't trying to do any more or any less. I really didn't bother with my classmates much. I stayed to myself and I liked it that way.

Everyone knew I was a huge Michael Jackson fan but I had no idea what my classmates had in store for me. They were having a meeting of the minds about me. All the girls in my class who knew Trisha were trying to hook the two of us up. They knew she dressed like Janet Jackson and danced like both Janet and Michael, so they really wanted us to meet. Queen, Tillenna, Racquel, Sonya, Sharon, Bow Bow were at the head of the whole thing. On Valentine's Day, February 14, 1990, my life would change and never be the same again. The girls in the class brought Trisha to our homeroom. They said, "Leon, there's someone at the door we 'd like you to meet." I went to

*Letter of Remebrance*

the door and what I saw would change me for life. She was beautiful! My God, she was a small little thing. Those eyes, those lips, it's you! I can feel it's you! All of this rushed through my head in a matter of seconds. She smiled and handed me a letter in an envelope freshly scented with her perfume. I had no idea that this young lady would have such an impact on my life. I had no idea what I was getting myself into. After that first day, she would write me letters on a daily basis. We would talk on the phone for what seemed like hours. We would write about our dreams and or feelings toward each other. We would talk about all the things that we had in common. It seemed too perfect. There were times I couldn't believe how compatible we actually were. At times it scared me a bit.

I had never met anyone who really lived life by the old saying "grab the bull by the horns." Trisha didn't let much hold her down and if she was down, she was back up before you even knew she was down. I loved that about her along with other qualities. She was always trying to tackle some dance step that

*Letter of Remebrance*

seemed difficult, practicing and practicing until she had the dance step right. Then, she would teach it to others. Nobody knew what to do or how to put together a dance routine like her. Trisha's talent never ceased to amaze me, even now.

"How do you do it with such ease and precision?" others would ask when she was teaching dance routines to kids at an area middle school for a school program. While her talent amazed me, I was equally in awe of her sensitivity and willingness to lend a helping hand to anyone in need. If you needed someone to talk to she was there to lend a listening ear and helpful words of encouragement.

Dancing was Trisha's love and her greatest dream was becoming a Star or a Star Choreographer. Looking back on Trisha's life, now, makes me realize just how important it is to follow your dreams, whatever they may be. Try not to get sidetracked from your dreams because time waits for no one. Don't be so eager to leave home early, thinking the grass is greener on the other side. There's a world out there, but it's not

*Letter of Remebrance*

*Earning My Wings*

always waiting for you with loving arms and a pat on the back. Sometimes when reality sets in, all you seem to get is a kick in the ass and a knife in the back. However, it's not always as hard as it seems. When you do the "right thing" like staying in school. If you do these things you won't have to settle for low paying jobs and finding yourself in jobs that degrade you or pull you down. Look for the type of work you can be proud of doing; something you know others respect and would be proud of you for doing. By striving to do the right thing, you show others that there is hope even when there seems like there is no hope at all. The jobs you might pick might not pay you the type of money you think you are worth, but, if it is honest and you put your faith in the right place, the right things will come your way. Life isn't always about WHO has acquired the most things; it's about HOW those things were acquired.

Honestly, don't put so much value on material things. Once you gain that inner peace and see that life is about much more than material things, you realize that your possessions don't

*Letter of Remebrance*

*Earning My Wings*

make up who you are inside. Then and only then will you see that your self-worth doesn't revolve around material things. Unfortunately, Trisha got caught up in a life of materialism and worldly gain. She was always a free spirit. She left home at such an early age, without finishing school, pursuing a path she thought would lead to her dream. But instead, it took her down the wrong path, away from her dream and towards a nightmare. By the time she realized that she needed to change her path because she had strayed off course, it was too late. (No, it's never too late. Even though Trisha dropped out of school, she did return to get her GED. You see, it's never too late.)

You see Trisha had a job that she wasn't proud of doing. The only reason that she kept the job was because it helped pay her bills. She started losing interest in the job and she decided to pull away and look elsewhere. It seemed hard for her in the beginning but she was starting to see it wasn't as hard as she had thought. Jobs were starting to fall into her lap and since she loved hair styling so much, she got a job doing just that.

*Letter of Remebrance*

*Earning My Wings*

Time seemed to get away for us, you see, we had lost touch for a few years. Our lives were both doing a total 360. We both had given each other space to grow. You know we were fairly young when we met and started dating. We didn't have any bad feelings toward each other, it was just one of those things. I'm glad we gave each other the space we needed in order to grow. It helped us to develop into the people that we were inside. Sometimes the person that you are inside adapts into a personality of its own. That's what helps you grow into yourself. When I sit back and analyze the situation, I realize that we needed to grow from the inside out. I am sure there have been times when you might have needed time and space away from your spouse or mate so that you could find out who you really are in hopes to reconnect. Sometimes it works and sometimes it does not. A lot of times you outgrow your mate. Meanwhile, back at the ranch, you come to see the differences

*Letter of Remebrance*

*Earning My Wings*

between relationships that are seasonal and others that are forever.

Lately, I have been having the same dream for the past three days and I can't seem to get it out of my head. I don't remember the dream too clearly, but I do remember that it has my old girlfriend, Trisha, in it and all these feelings seem to be building up inside of me. I've never dreamed about her before. Maybe it's nothing or maybe I should call her or go see her. I don't know I don't know why I am blowing this out of proportion, it's probably nothing. After all it's just a dream. Dreams don't' mean anything. I don't have all day to sit here thinking about some dream; pulling my hair out trying to figure out the particulars of a dream. Anyway, I am running late for work. Shit! I hope that I didn't miss my bus. Man, I did miss my bus. I thought I heard a bus going up the street. By the time I finally made it to the bus stop, the next bus I saw coming up the street wasn't even in service. Thank goodness I finally made it to work. It seemed as if I would never get there. You know, I'm

*Letter of Remebrance*

always running to get to work. I don't know why but I've been thinking about my old girlfriend. Just thinking about Trisha always makes me smile. She always had a weird sense of humor and could find humor in some of the craziest of things.

I can't seem to get her off my mind; the laughter, the jokes, and that smile. This wasn't making any sense to me. I did not know what to look for, and not only that but what to say if I saw her. Yet, I am sure the words will come. At 10:45 p.m., close to quitting time at work, I decide I'll catch a cab to her house since it is pouring down raining outside and tell her how much I love her, miss her and want her in my life. Then I think, NO! I'll walk in the rain, that's what I'll do. I'll show her that I am crazy in love enough to walk in the rain, through a storm. I looked out the window at the storm and regained my senses. Hell No! I am not walking case closed. I am not walking in nobody's rain sorry that's not going to work. Then it hit me, wait a minute I thought, I am supposed to be cool, right? Yeah, if you're cool you don't do all that for any girl, do you? But it occurs to me

*Letter of Remebrance*

*Earning My Wings*

that this girl isn't just any girl. Oh no, this is Patricia, and I don't care what other people think I am going to get my girl if that's the last thing I ever do. Because of the history we had together, I couldn't let it go. She was the type of girl that was truly one in a million and that alone was the only explanation why I can't let her get away.

At 11:30 p.m. I'm getting ready to punch the clock and go home right after I figure out what happened to my backpack. I know I put it in this chair now where did it go. I asked one of my co-workers if she had seen my bag and she said you know that girl that works on your floor on the night shift. You know the one with the braids. "What" I replied. She was mumbling something about you left some work for her to do, I took off like a bullet where is she oh there she is where is my bag? She said you forgot to do A, B, C, I said is that all! After I zoomed through all that I was going to do I kindly told her as only I could using every expletive I could think of and then I was on my way. I ran down to the clock to punch out. The rain was

*Letter of Remebrance*

really coming down. I made it to the bus stop and met up with a fellow co-worker. We started talking for a few minutes, about what I don't know! While he was talking I was busy thinking about other things, my mind somewhere else. A second or two later, I thought I was seeing things. Is that Trisha? What is she doing up here? She pulled off the road into the loop area where the bus pulls up. I didn't believe what I was seeing. No, it couldn't be but some how I knew it was true. It was her. My heart told me GO! GO! GO! I instantly ran up to the car and got in not even thinking it might not be her. But, when I saw that face I knew. I was a little out of breath after I ran to the car even though I hadn't run that far. None the less, my heart felt so good to be in her presence again. I was just thinking about you.

It was odd because when I started talking to her, it didn't seem as though we had been away from each other for as long as we had. It was just like we picked up where we left off. She told me she was looking for the house of one of her girlfriends, which is why she was in the area. However, I knew better than

*Letter of Remebrance*

that. God brought her here on this night for a reason. Only he knew the reason for this meeting. She said she wasn't real familiar with this part of town and I guess she thought I could help her. Unfortunately, I did not know anymore than she did, so I wasn't much help. So we pulled off from the bus stop and headed to the gas station so she could use the pay phone and call for directions. While I waited in the car, I started to daydream about the last time I was in a car with Patricia.

*I was working at a local motel in the area about a few miles away from where we were parked* now. *The motel was having its annual Christmas party and I* had *invited Trisha to come. After we left the party, we headed downtown to make a few stops* before heading home. *I don't remember what street we were on downtown but Trisha started going up a one way street in the middle of traffic. I didn't realize it was one way at*

*Letter of Remebrance*

*Earning My Wings*

*first, but trust me, we found out soon enough. I started panicking but she stayed calm and started laughing.*

*"How can you laugh at a time like this," I yelled.*

*"Boy, everything is going to be okay. Sit back and relax," she grinned.*

*"I can't relax at a time like this," I said.*

*"I know what I am doing," she continued.*

*"Well, I can't tell! I am getting out of this car, Trisha. Girl, I got to get OUT! The police are going to take us to jail.*

*"You act like the car is stolen or something," she said.*

*"No, I know it's not stolen, but you ain't killing me in this car!*

*Just then, we heard sirens. The police pull up behind us with their lights blinking and everything. "You don't' need to be driving," I said.*

*"Shut up, Leon!" she said getting out of the car to*

*Letter of Remebrance*

*talk to the police officer.*

*I started mumbling to myself. She can't talk to me like that I don't know who she thinks she is. If you can't drive you can't drive. I don't know what she's talking about she missed the signs that read "ONE WAY." I started frantically looking for my ID. I did not want them to think that we were in a stolen car or anything. Trisha got back into the car.*

*"Everything is fine"*

*"Really," I said in disbelief.*

*"Yes, I told you it would be now calm your little nerves we are not going to jail"*

*"NO?"*

*After that was said and done, we headed home. Come to find out, it really wasn't her car like I thought it was. She had borrowed it from a friend. I leaned over and whispered in her ear, you know I am too pretty to go to jail. She looked at me eye to eye and we were both*

*Letter of Remebrance*

*laughing. Through it all, Trisha was calm and cool every step of the way. Things were working out just fine and the night had come to a peaceful end.*

Trisha comes back from the pay phone and I woke up from my trance. She said forget it. Forget looking for it! I am not looking for this girl's house. I am going home, so she gave me a lift home and we talked along the way. There were so many things that I wanted to talk about and it seemed like I had so little time to do it. Every minute seemed like a second, as if time was speeding up. I had just left a job where I was on the clock and when I got into her car, it seemed like the clock started up again. I had to pour out my heart in a matter of seconds because I didn't know when I was going to see her again. I needed to tell her exactly how I felt. I asked her when I was going to see her again and she said I don't know. I'm off work Saturday and Sunday, maybe Saturday we could go out, I offered. She said call me and smiled. I took that as I would see her, even though it would be

*Letter of Remebrance*

*Earning My Wings*

the last time I would be in her company, at least just the two of us together.

The Saturday afternoon that I had been waiting for came and Trisha came over to my house. She hadn't been in my house for years. We sat on my bed in my room talking about old times and all the fun we had. I had such a good feeling when I started looking in her eyes. Every gesture brought back memories, all good memories. Trying to recapture all those wonderful memories from over the years can be like pulling up an anchor from a deep ocean. It's so deep since it's been in the ocean for years that it's hard even to smile at the good times. That's all I can seem to remember are the good times.

*Once in a downtown mall inside a restaurant a few years earlier, we sat only a few feet away together eating Chinese food. I had shrimp fried rice and she had the mixed vegetables. My, my, my, time sure does get away when you're having fun. I always would*

*Letter of Remebrance*

*remember Trisha was busy and engulfed in life. There always was something she was doing or getting ready to do. Finishing something, hurrying to get to somewhere to buy something that she would only wear once, late for something or trying to figure out where it was. That's my baby, but you know, through all of that she made time for family and close friends.*

Trisha said she was a little hungry and wanted a salad, so I went downstairs to ask my mom to make her a salad. I am sure she would say no problem.

"Ma, could you fix a salad for Trisha?

"Sure," she said, "I'll make one for her."

As little as Trisha was she sure could eat believe it or not, even though she was eating a salad. She could throw down with some food. Trust me, she wasn't going to starve for no one. The girl could eat.

"I didn't mean to bother you Ma. I know you're busy, down

*Letter of Remebrance*

here working on one of your many projects in the basement."

"Whatever, Lee," she replied.

Later, I asked Trisha if she could give me a ride to the mall after she finished eating the salad. She said sure because she had a few runs to make anyway. But before I got out the car I needed to ask a very important question that had been on my mind for a long time.

"Do you still love me?" I asked.

"Why did you ask me that? You know the answer. I'll always love you," she responded.

I softly kissed her cheek and said I still love you too. At that moment I understood the truth in saying that time waits for no one. Even though I tried to wait for you while you were out there doing everything that you were big and bad enough to do. I was still living in the past and we had grown apart. I stood and watched her pull off the lot at the mall where she had dropped me off I felt in my heart that we would not have too many encounters like that anymore. Life had really changed us both.

*Letter of Remebrance*

*Earning My Wings*

Where are those two kids who were madly in love? Where are they? They are at the bottom of the ocean with the Hope Diamond.

She was one of those types I just couldn't imagine what she would be like in 30-40 years. Some people you can see what they could probably be like as they age but Trisha, her beauty would be timeless and she would never age.

You had a certain flair for the creative. You created your own style for dress and hair. You always had a way of making a not so good outfit into an unbelievable outfit with special add-ons. You always would go above and beyond to show people that you were there for them, family and friends alike. I remembered a few days earlier when I spoke to your Mom we recalled many particular situations you showed extra-special concern for us. All the love you had to show from surprise limousine rides at the door to surprise visits at the house with just a kiss in mind. Even when your sisters and brothers needed your special care, concern and love, you were there to brighten

*Letter of Remebrance*

*Earning My Wings*

their mornings, evenings and nights.

I was so lucky to be one of her close friends I don't understand why it had to be you. Why you? There are so many things that happen because God wants it to and you have no control over it. I wrote a poem that helps me remember her. The poem is title; "I AM MISSING YOU." I know you are probably sick of hearing about Trisha this and Trisha that, but you'll get over it.

As for me, I am still finding things to hold onto when it comes to you. You made me feel so wanted and so loved. You made me feel life was worth living because you were in my life. I keep trying to find people to replace you but your are irreplaceable. I never thought losing you would have such an affect on my life but you did. There's nothing I wouldn't do to have a kiss from you. Kissing you made my life worth living. Nothing could compare to your kiss.

Do you believe in magic? What about miracles? What about true friendship? Patricia was all those things and a whole

*Letter of Remebrance*

lot more. To know her was to love her. Trisha, there could never be another you. When I first met you I was so young and naive. I didn't know what love was. I had never been with a girl until you. You broke down all of the insecurities I had about girls. You were thoughtful and caring. Sometimes you gave when you really did not have to give. I thank you for being you. It was you who introduced me to a side of Michael Jackson's music I had never heard. I did not realize then, but the music that you had acquainted me with was really music describing your life, your insecurities. You made me feel like there was nothing in this world that I couldn't do. I thank you for helping me tear down those walls I had put up my whole life. You showed me that there was more to you, than just a pretty face. You were deeper than that. Knowing and loving you enabled me to face my own insecurities and encouraged me not be ashamed of who I was and not to hide behind walls. In remembering that Bible phrase *"Better is he that is in me than he that is in the world."*

TO THE BEREAVED FAMILY

*Letter of Remebrance*

I just want to say a little something to let you know the Patricia Ann Melton I knew:

I never thought the day would come when I would be standing before all of you under the circumstances that bring us here tonight. Trisha my love for you will never fade.

It would take more time than this service allows for me to explain all the wonderful things that best describe Trisha. Nothing can compare to her bubbly sparkling personality. Her smile and laughter will endure in all who knew her.

I know one of Patricia's many dreams was to become a star, but stars come and go. I just want you to know this. Trisha, every night when I look to the heavens, I'll see you, sparkling and shining like only true stars do!

Be special to someone, it can make a difference in his or her life. Forgive everyone of everything and, in turn, God will forgive you!

*Letter of Remebrance*

*Earning My Wings*

(Trisha departed this life on May 7, 1999 as a victim of handgun violence, murdered heinously.)

*Letter of Remebrance*

## Diary Page: Misled By Lust

I had no idea of what lay in store for me. Never in my wildest dreams would I ever expect for my mother to put me out. I always knew that my mother was a sneak, it comes with the title mother. Which means your business is my business because you have no business at all as far as she is concerned especially if it is under her roof. That is one of the most famous lines in the world, "not under my roof." To what extreme she would go, however, I did not know or when she would strike, I had no clue. They say you go looking for trouble you just might find it. After I discovered that my mother had gone through my personal belongings and found something among them that she thought she would never see in my possession, that was the icing on the cake. She had also been reading through my journal entries on my desk in my bedroom. I found out quick, fast and in a hurry who my true friends were and what family members were in my corner.

*Diary Page*

*Earning My Wings*

When my mother said she would put me out, I could count my friends and family on one hand. I stayed at a close friend's for a week until my cousin agreed to let me stay at her house and how many of you know, it was not for free. Family or no family, if you want to eat you have to pay; all that other shit gets the boot.

I lived such a sheltered life growing up with my mother and stepfather. I am almost certain that they might even try to debate that fact, but that is truly how I felt. It did not make me feel good at all. The other kids made me feel as if there was something wrong with me because I was not able to do all the things they could do such as going on the field trips and other places of that nature. For my entire life, it seems that I have been trying to fit in with the guy next door but some how that was the hardest thing to do. I have always wanted to go to my parents and ask them for their input in my life but they always had the wrong attitude for the situation, leaving me feeling

*Diary Page*

distant from them. I felt that I was in this world all alone, truly all alone and when I would ask my parents something it was like talking to a wall. After a while their attitude started to take its toll on me and the people around me. I did not see it coming but I was slowly starting to find myself in the company of all kinds of people I had never been around before. I found myself in self degrading situations on a regular basis and not having a problem with it. It did not take much for me to be misled by my peers. I wanted to be in with the "in-crowd" and at those times I was going through desperate times trying to find myself. What I was really finding was how to be like everybody else and far from who I really was. I had no idea who I was. Anything that didn't seem normal was what attracted me. I felt so different and, of course, when you have people telling you that you are different, that in itself can make you or brake you. I wanted to do things that were not the norm. I was around people who thought life was a big joke; a fucking party. Everything was built on sex and

*Diary Page*

*Earning My Wings*

image and those things were not the norm for me, but it was for them, and I was right in the thick of it.

When I made the sudden move to my cousin's house, I thought I would lose my mind. I got more than I bargained for. I understood that I was living in a two story, two bedroom, one bath row house with between nine other people. It was nerve racking, to say the least. For the first time in my life I was out on my own, but let me tell you, it wasn't all peaches and cream. All the way through, I had to come up with the money to pay my cousin. I did not want to, but I knew that wherever I went I would have to pay sooner or later. Since I had no money, my grandfather gladly offered me money to hold me over. One other close friend, whom I had known for years, offered to help and stood by me until I was able to pay my own way. For that I am forever thankful.

After I was able to get on my feet and do for myself, I started to spread my wings a bit. I was at a club every night and loving it. I was going from city to city to city, partying it up. I was

*Diary Page*

*Earning My Wings*

living the fast life. I was deeply deprived as a young child and young adult, so the one thing that I thought that I wanted to do was to go to clubs and party with kids my age. I was not into drinking because it wasn't my style. My mother did not allow me to spend the kind of time I wanted to with my friends. I am sure that she was not really aware of how overly protective she really was, but like everything else you do for a long enough time, you start to get use to it. I adapted to coming home after school. While other kids were outside having fun, I was in the house looking at the latest soap opera, waiting for it to go off only to sit in front of the TV and watching something else. Other times, I would sit with a big bowl of popcorn looking at *Oprah* trying to do my homework at the same time. This is what I did when I lived at home with my Mom.

Well, the time had arrived for me to come face to face with the one thing I had never done, go to a Gay Club. I just could not believe what I was seeing. Men dancing together, everybody just so happy and "Gay." I really was not ready for that. The

*Diary Page*

*Earning My Wings*

one thing that I liked was the fact that there was a unity there that I had never felt. I thought it was attractive to see people being themselves. When the night was over, I had to face the real world once more, bills had to be paid and at that time my cousin was working very hard to make ends meet. I went job searching all around town. I got up early in the morning because that is the way I was raised. If there is an able body in the house you get up and looked for a job. I made a few phone calls and got a response from a local motel in Pikesville, Maryland that was looking for housekeepers. I was working in a matter of days and the days turned into years. What a blessing that was for me, knowing I would not have to rely on anyone to help me pay my way.

At my age it was important for me to take control of my life before life took control of me. Having a full time job meant more time at work and less time going out to the clubs but some way, some how, I made time to do it all. I even had a girlfriend. She would come over a lot; it seemed like she had moved in

*Diary Page*

because she never went home. Sometimes she would get on my nerves, I felt like she was crowding me. Don't get me wrong, I loved her and all the attention but I liked my privacy too. As a child I had always had a lot of time to myself to think things over and I found myself fighting between my love for my girlfriend and privacy for myself.

I was also fighting my deep hidden sexual desires for the same sex. Believe it or not, both types of desires and relationships were very new to me. Same sex or opposite sex, I had not started having sex of any kind until I was 19 years old. I was very inexperienced in the area of sexuality. It was extremely hard for me to have to deal with other men trying get with my girl or hearing them trying to discredit me and my manhood in order to win over my girlfriend. They would say that I was not worthy of her and that they could make her feel better than I could. This hurt because she had been the only girl that I had let into my world mentally, sexually.

I am not really sure when or how, but things never really

*Diary Page*

*Earning My Wings*

worked out between us. Sometimes, I wish that they did but then other times I am glad that they did not. All the things that I was going through were growing periods for me right down to the letter. I have been in a cross between love and infatuation with sexual partners many times after her, but my true deep rooted love for her still remains. I knew at a time when uncertainty ruled the air and everything was still new to see and to taste. Patricia Ann Melton, I'll always love you.

Time went on and I started experimenting. I knew I liked girls, but I had a strange sexual desire for men. I was at a stand still. I did not want to choose between the two but I did not know what to do or what was the right move to make. Should I be thinking what is the politically correct move to make? Well, you know what this is don't you. Homosexuality is wrong and you are going to hell if you are gay, we all know that. It's right up there with God made Adam and Eve, not Adam and Steve. I was sure that wasn't the right move for me at this time in my life. What would people think if they knew the me inside. I

*Diary Page*

*Earning My Wings*

wanted to be the me that I had been hiding. How would they treat me? The problems that came along with coming out of the closet could go one or two ways and I did not know which way it would go for me. I knew that it could be horrible and embarrassing to both me and my family, especially my mother. Somehow getting far away from home became my number one priority. My passion for the same sex over rode any other logical decision that I had to face in my life at that time. I just knew that out there was where I wanted to be. It was hard to live up to the expectations that my mother had for me; expectations that only a brain surgeon could live up to. I guess I was really not mature enough at that time to really take life seriously.

I fell into a life style of bisexuality, not accepting the choice of being either fully gay or fully straight. Feeling and not acknowledging one preference over another made my head spin in confusion. I felt as if the more I surrounded myself with my own insecurities, the more my true self came through. I felt more secure with what I was doing and how I was living but

*Diary Page*

*Earning My Wings*

there were still times when I thought that I did not make the right decisions on how to live my life. I wanted to run away from the feelings but wherever I would go they would be there following me ... hounding me ... driving me and my reactions. I started to blame any and everything to detract the true feelings that I had inside. I was afraid my homosexuality was a figment of my imagination, a phase that would soon pass. It was manifested and made real for me by the people I selected to hang around. I would think, so that is why I have the feelings that I do, they are not real.

Well, I soon found out that they were real. Perhaps, before I really was not ready because I knew that to live a gay life would change me in many ways. But I also know that blame is not the answer; it just makes the truth much more easier to deal with. Truth in ourselves is something that is hard to deal with when you are in denial. You are not always the same as the company you keep, it all depends on the individual and what his or her expectations of themselves are and what they want out of the

*Diary Page*

*Earning My Wings*

situation that they are in.

The day of truth came on March 18, 1993. I had called my mother but when she answered the phone it caught me off guard. She said she wanted to talk to me, in a way you really did not know what to expect. Me and your father. I was on pins and needles. I was not sure if I wanted to go but I went. When I got to the door, my stomach was doing flips. I was so nervous. I rang the bell and my mother came down and opened the door. I did not know what to expect. I was surely not going to get a hug, that was truly out of the question. I walked over to the dining room and when I got to the dining table I did not know whether to sit or stand. I was at a lost for words. I sat at the head of the table. I felt like a stranger in my own house since I had been gone so long. It was an eerie feeling, like time had stood still and every minute was an hour. When we started talking I got defensive only because my mother always had a way of being too honest at the wrong time about things that should not be the topic of discussion. She had an innate gift for

*Diary Page*

*Earning My Wings*

picking you apart and leaving your scraps along the side of the road for the vultures. It really made me mad when she did that and I was starting to think of how ridiculous this meeting was. I did not like being put on the spot, but I knew I would have to be but I did not have to like it. The hardest thing was telling my mother, to her face, that I wanted to have a relationship with a man. That I am a homosexual.

I guarantee you she was not ready for what I said. Those words gave me some kind of freedom. No matter how hurtful it was then, like wild flowers, all my personal business was spread through the whole family like a plague. It did not take long for relatives that I thought I was close to, to write me off. They turned their backs on me. I did not realize that saying you want to be with a man would gain so much attention. Some of my family members did not take the news well and retaliated against my mother. I guess that she was not expecting that they would cut her down and say shameful things to her nasty comments. I forgive them but I'll never forget. No one is perfect, it's always

*Diary Page*

*Earning My Wings*

the unjust telling the just how to live in this unjust world where sin hovers over like the clouds above. There is only one true judge of the life styles we live and things we say and do and it is not man. Only Christ knows all answers to our vast questions. A time will come when order will rule under a new leadership and in that world is where I'd like to be. Under my Father's care of perfect understanding, where others in the worldly world can't understand. "Let he who is without sin cast the first stone!"

*Diary Page*

## Diary Page: Sugar Candy and Mints

It was the year 1987; I was still in junior high school and confused about my career goals and aspirations. I was one step away from the eighth grade and waiting for graduation day. At this time of my life, it seemed as though I had so many struggles to contend with. I was still in my early teens and still enjoying the things that kids my age enjoyed; like watching wrestling on TV on Saturday afternoons. I stayed glued to the TV playing video games and having all around fun.

When I think about my family from adolescence to young adulthood, we seemed to be pretty close. I had aunts, uncles, and grandparents. all of who lived within a 15-20 mile radius. I never had to worry about not having a family member close by. The only relative that lived beyond the 20-mile radius was my great-great aunt, Ms. Ethel Moore. I rarely saw Aunt Etha, as I called her, except when we went to church on Sunday mornings. She was one of the last of my grandfather's older sisters and in

*Diary Page*

*Earning My Wings*

her late 70s, early 80s. While she always treated me with loving-kindness, I had heard other family members say that in her day she was a real whippersnapper. They recalled that if she lifted her hand, you knew she wasn't putting it out for a handshake, you'd better get ready for a slap upside your head, with the quickness. But a lot of those things changed over the years. Times were changing and there were certain things that you just didn't do anymore. It seemed that the quickest hand had become a thing of the past. But to this day, I am sure she had one of the quickest hands in the business when it came to slapping you upside your head.

As a child, I always remember my aunt sitting in one of the first four rows of the church. Whenever she saw my mother and I come into the church, she would always motion for me to come sit with her in the front of the church. My mom would always let me go. I liked sitting with my auntie mainly because she had all the treats in her purse. She always had that sugar candy in her purse and who could forget those hard mints. They could

*Diary Page*

*Earning My Wings*

choke a cow, but I loved them none-the-less. I remember sitting on her lap or just sitting close to her whenever I saw her. She made me feel happy. However, she would make me cringe when she would spit ... clean my glasses. After she did that my glasses had a stinky smell ... yuck yuck yucky!

My stepfather's mother only lived a few blocks away from Aunt Etha, so whenever we went to her house, I would always be inclined to go to see my Aunt Etha. She would always say, "don't let me have to come up there and get you. You are my nephew, come see me whenever you want, anytime." Just writing about you Aunt Etha makes me miss her even more.

I remember going to her house and having long talks with her in the kitchen. I don't remember too much of what we talked about; all I know is we always had something to talk about. I also remember making my favorite peanut butter and jelly sandwiches. I always loved putting lots of jelly on the bread to the point where the jelly was coming out on either side. You guessed it, making a mess in the kitchen over peanut butter and

*Diary Page*

*Earning My Wings*

jelly was lots of fun. Our visit wasn't complete unless I was making a mess.

In addition to our talks and making a mess in the kitchen, I was always enjoyed going to her house because it was just like visiting a museum. Walking through room after room where she had beautiful antique clocks, a shiny silver tea set, beautiful dishes and antique furniture on display. A shiny crystal chandelier hung from the ceiling in the dining room and antique rugs adorned the floors of the living room and dining room. I was captivated by the beautiful antique surroundings and didn't know whether to sit or take pictures. So most of the time, I made my way to the kitchen because everything was right at my fingertips and I didn't have to worry about messing up anything.

Unfortunately, my aunt and I lost touch for number of years. There were no real reasons why we hadn't kept in touch. The only thing I could think of was that I had grown older and was now in my early teens. Ripping and running around town as most teens do, a lot of time I forgot to call or to take the time to

*Diary Page*

*Earning My Wings*

go see her. Don't get me wrong, I still loved my Auntie. My love for her never faded, but the desire to sit on her lap during church service faded. It had become a thing of the past. Sugar candy and mints weren't the first things I thought of on Sunday morning any more. But when I heard the news that my favorite Aunt had taken ill, my heart had dropped and it hit me like a ton of bricks. No! No! It can't be! Not my Aunt Etha!

I knew that my Aunt Etha was up in age, but I didn't put too much thought into the reality of what that meant in terms of life and living. I was not interested in learning about loved ones I cared about dying and never returning, I don't think that would of sat too well with me as a topic of conversation. When I found out that my beloved Aunt had taken ill, I was disturbed by the awful things I heard about how she was being treated. On more than one occasion, she had to fight-off rough handlers in the nursing homes and hospitals. It seems she was speaking fine until she entered the nursing home, but subsequently, there was talk of some kind of abuse that took place there. The last time I

*Diary Page*

*Earning My Wings*

would ever see my Aunt alive was while she was still in the hospital. My mother and I went to the hospital to see how she was doing. She did not have any tubes coming from her nor did she have any IV or respiratory tubing on her. But the one thing that I noticed as being wrong was that she was so quiet. She would open and close her eyes and look around not really fixing them on anything in particular. My mother asked her in a quiet way if she would like to have your hair combed. "I'll braid it so it's not looking so wild," my mother whispered. After braiding her hair, my mom said, "your feet are a little cold, so to help the circulation, I'll rub them a bit." I stood at the window looking up to the sky and closed my eyes for a second or two. "What can I do?" I cried to myself. I felt so helpless and empty inside. I could not look at her. Everytime I looked at her I kept asking "Why? Why?, Why would someone do such a thing?" I felt this burning in the pit of my stomach. How could anyone harm such a weak old lady to the extent that she could not speak anymore? In my heart, I ached so much to give her a kiss but I was so

*Diary Page*

*Earning My Wings*

afraid of showing my emotions. I had so much to hide. I didn't want to show my vulnerable side and I really did not want my mother to see me cry. I did not feel that was something that I could express yet, but I made a vow that one day I will work for a hospital and I will be the eyes, ears, and voice of the patients who were mistreated or left unattended or who were just ignored. I would be there to fill the cups of those who could not help themselves or who might just need someone to hold the cup so they could drink. Little did I know that my prayers would be answered. I did in fact get a job when I turned 22 at a hospital, and helping people in need has been a gift within itself.

*Diary Page*

# Remembrance: Your Calling

The question is always asked, what is my purpose? Why am I here? Why am I on this planet? These are the questions we ask ourselves. We want to know our calling. I have run across so many life experiences which is normal to do for normal experiences, that is, but in my everyday life everything seems to be an adventure. From waking up, leaving to go wherever, to coming back something unusual seems to happen to me. It doesn't amaze me anymore because it has become routine, an everyday occurrence like taking a skip to the bathroom. But, it's a damn shame because that is no kind real settled life. It's the unexplained situation, the something for which you have no real answers. You know, something that you feel in your gut that happens because God wanted it to and wanted you to be aware that, yes, this is happening and no, it can't be explained. Its meant to be, its your calling, the calling of your life.

*Remembrance*

*Earning My Wings*

So put the gear in motion and make magic; make things happen; bring things together as only you know how; complimenting both sides at the same time. I have asked myself time and time again why it was you but I still have no answers. Why did we share the bond that we did in the way we did without even knowing one another? It has to be the old adage, when people say that I have known you before in another life, another time, another millennium or a time long ago. And we managed to find each other again and share what we had before, the closeness, a bond that seemed to have stood the test of time and space. I felt honored to have the job I did not know what lay in store for me but I would find out I had nothing to prepare me for the job or did I? You know time is of the essence and you must make the most of the time you have with the ones you love because in a twinkling of an eye they are gone. So take advantage of the precious time we have while the time is allowed. I am so thankful that I was given a chance to know and

*Remembrance*

*Earning My Wings*

help one of God's children in dire need of true love, honesty, trust and companionship. These things could not come true at a better time for the right person who did not know he would be in as much need as he was and as well as for me, not knowing I would be willing and able to meet all the necessary needs of this particular individual without complaint, only longing to help comfort, love, protect, extinguish all worry, stress in my power.

Leon Lynn Thomas Jr., Tavon was what he loved to be called. While he was in the hospital for an evaluation, he regretfully found out that he would need to have major surgery. After surgery, he was in so much pain. He had moments when he had a tube in his nose that along with the operation, he was weak all over very helpless and in distress. I don't think that he was really ready for what was happening to him as quickly as it did. Seeing some of his old acquaintances that he had not seen in a long time, was very comforting to him. A few laughs and lots of hugs and kisses, trying to kiss away the pain when you are going through tough times in your life. And in Tavon's case the

*Remembrance*

*Earning My Wings*

tough times were just beginning and true friends were just too far and few. If you were one of the far and few, you were chosen because he wanted you to be around him and if he didn't want you to be around him, believe you me, you'd know! He would come right out and tell you.

I'll never forget how we met. It seemed like the tables were turning before I had even saw him. He was already hearing things about me; what I looked like and how much he favored the guy who worked at the hospital on the same floor as his room. I remember strolling down the hall when I saw him. I walked pass Room 213 quickly and then I walked back. I just had to get another look and then he spoke.

"Hey you."

"Who me?"I replied.

"Yeah, come here."

I slowly walked into the room and looked at him. What a sight to behold. It was like looking at a brother that I never had.

"What's your name?"

*Remembrance*

"It's Leon, what's yours."

"Leon, too. You must be the guy everybody wanted me to meet. I see why. You look like me when I was younger. When you get my age you are going to look like me."

He would always say that. However, I was not quite ready for this. But, I noticed that as we started talking, it seemed as if we had known one another before. Just like we were old acquaintances picking up where we left off. When it was time for me to go home that evening, I couldn't wait to tell my best friend and have them speak to each other. So many things had happened in such a short time. It was truly unreal and now I am sitting in remembrance. It is so hard to believe Leon had a major operation that left him sick for the majority of the time we spent together.

I found myself spending the night in the hospital because I was so concerned about his treatment. Sometimes, nurses don't always come running when you need them and sometimes you

*Remembrance*

*Earning My Wings*

need some one there who will give them the extra push to get the job done. If they don't come, you have someone there who will be there if you need some help. I stayed for only two nights, but those two nights seemed to never end. Even though I knew I would have to go to work the same day, I did it and would do it again.

I would be half awake and half asleep trying to make sure that I did not miss anything as I sat in a chair holding his hand as he slowly drifted off to sleep. I tried to sleep on another occasion on a cot because he would tell me that I looked uncomfortable before when I was sleeping sitting up in the chair and he said I should lay down. I did not want to because I did not want to leave his side but I did because I was a little uncomfortable in that chair. I did not let anything pass by my eyes, that did not have to because he wanted me there and I knew that for sure. I know you might think that I seemed to be a little over concerned but Tavon would always ask me to stay. If you could see the look in his eyes, the fear of you leaving, you would

*Remembrance*

*Earning My Wings*

know that staying is what you would have to do. That is why I was so concerned. I did not want him to be in anymore pain than necessary at that time.

Since I worked in the hospital, I knew I would have to go to work soon. I dreaded going but when I went I would be in constant worry I missed him so. Tavon was like a big brother to me. He would always make me laugh, he was so funny. I just didn't want anyone to upset him, in his condition getting upset was not something that we wanted. People would always say he is spoiled and that I was adding to it but I couldn't see that at the time. Nor was it something that I cared to discuss at that time. When it was being told to me, I knew that he needed a different kind of caring for and I knew that I was the only one that could give it to him.

All of our long talks helped me realize how much of a good friend, I had become to Tavon. He often expressed to me about what a friend we had in each other and how much we needed each other I did not care who saw that we were close friends and

*Remembrance*

we openly showed our affection toward each other. He taught me to never be apprehensive of showing your true feelings in situations concerning love, friendship, family. You just have to have a touch of class when it comes to situations; not try to be someone you are not. Putting up walls, worrying about every opinion of you and the friends you pick was not worth it. Everyone is not going to like everyone you call friend or brother or lover.

As uncomfortable as I was in public, he was not, which soon showed me how much I meant to him. The same emotions he showed me in the hospital room were the same he showed me outside the hospital room. I did not expect for him to be real, I thought that he was going to be fake and phoney, and that he was not. Yes, he could put away all the insecurities that would attach themselves to two men, especially when one man looks like he might be gay. People are always trying to but things together and even if they are wrong it does not make them any never mind. People are going to be people, no matter what the

*Remembrance*

*Earning My Wings*

situation. After all, everyone is entitled to their opinion.

I had never meet anyone quite like Tavon or his mother and the rest of his family and friends. They were like the icing on the cake. I was at a cross roads in my life and I was trying to pull away from the things I had been involved in the past. Things that were leading me down a path of destruction or near death. When I would come to Tavon mom's house, she was always so kind and loving. She took a special liking to me. I don't know why but she did.

Mother is what we all called her. She was always ready to prepare you something to eat; cooking was her forte. If she was not cooking for herself or her family, she was cooking for somebody else. But trust me, she made time for her Bingo. She would take regular trips to Atlantic City to play Bingo when she could find the time. I guess it relaxed her along with being with old friends. But cooking was her heart. She could whip up something in a flash and don't tell her that you aren't hungry, that's just like telling her that you are hungry and are too shy to

*Remembrance*

ask for something to eat. Well, I tried that a few times. I would say I am not hungry and God knows I was and she would look at me and say okay. In a few minutes, she would be back with a plate of food in her hands. She did not mess around and I loved her for it with every bite. Mother was a generous kind, sweet woman who was always ready to lend a helping hand. She had the kind of down home, open arms, welcoming you into her arms mentality that you don't see everyday. Only in old movies. If there were more people like mother, I am sure this world would be a better place. A little bit of love can go a long way, especially when it is homemade.

When I was ill and needed a mother's care a mother who was not my own comforted me with her mothering instincts and did her best to nurse me well. It was so hard because she had so many other things to contend with, but through it all she helped me plenty. Her son was battling for his life. To lose him was just too much for the heart of a mother and it was to much for a son to leave his mother. Tavon was on so many different kinds

*Remembrance*

*Earning My Wings*

of medications that we could not even name, so many different times to take them it was so confusing for him to understand and me too. It was so nerve racking for him he tried to understand the different times and dosages but it was impossible for either of us. I did all that I could and he knew I wanted to do more but there was only so much I could do. It was so hard to see a 32-year old man go from a strong-hearted, fearless lion to a withdrawn sickly man who's temper would flare up in an instant. Many nights he would wake up in a deep sweat or he just could not sleep at all which was very hard for him to deal with. His eyes were blood shot, his stomach was in knots, constant pain and discomfort was his companion. All I could do was hold his hand ad lend a helping hand.

Tavon worried about so many things. One of them was death. How could you not worry about death. But he also worried about his mother. She worked two jobs and would get up early in the morning and not get back until late at night. Catching the bus in rain, sleet, snow, sun, she was truly a

*Remembrance*

*Earning My Wings*

trooper. Mother was dealing with her son's sickness and she need someone to look out for her also.

We all encouraged her to go to the hospital and have a doctor see her but she did not want to do that even though she knew her bronchitis was starting to get the best of her. She had a terrible cold, coughing and bringing up mucus sometimes on occasion. One afternoon we were entertaining a close friend and I was running a little late for work, so I left Tavon and my friend and went to work. From what was told to me by Tavon's mom, they were having a conversation about how Tavon wanted her to go to the hospital. He begged and pleaded with her but mother declined. Well, Tavon just lost it, for a few minutes. This was a side of her son she had not seen before. He had never talked to her like that before and it shocked and hurt her. Of course, Tavon apologized to mother and he was very sorry for the way he acted.

It still strikes me at times when ever I think about his temper at this time of his life, he must have been fighting with himself thus fighting with others. When my grandfather was ill, Tavon

*Remembrance*

*Earning My Wings*

was always in my corner lending a supporting listening ear or helping hand. Well, when my PopPop passed away I was besides myself and Tavon was very supportive. My PopPop was my whole world in so many ways. I loved that old man. When the time came for his funeral, I was not ready. There was no way that I could ever be ready for something like and I started becoming physically ill.

I later found out I had the strep throat and I was in so much pain my throat felt like hell. I became light headed and I hadn't eaten in days. To top it all off, when I found out about the death of my PopPop, I stopped eating all together. Tavon tried to get me to eat. I knew he was going through so much himself, but now I was the one who needed the attention and care. I could see the distress on his face, he just could not stand to see me in a helpless distressful way. But all in all, I eventually pulled things together by the Grace of God.

Tavon had so much on his mind, he knew that time was winding down. He never came to me and said anything about

*Remembrance*

his own death or about his views of what lay ahead at the end of the road. Never would he tell me of such things and you know I don't think that I would have been ready for that kind of a conversation, especially from someone that meant so much to me. Just knowing that I would lose them soon, sooner than I thought, and that I'd never see again among the land of the living was hard enough to bare. Tavon was going to the hospital regularly to have his blood cleaned with blood transfusions; take the old out and put new in. I prayed that his was good blood and not defective. Tavon was very uncomfortable about going out to certain places because he had two transfusion tubes sticking out of his neck. It was very uncomfortable for him, not just because it was very unattractive, but because he really had a hard time sleeping with the tubes poking out the side of his neck.

After Tavon found out about the death of my PopPop, he told me that he would like to come to the funeral in support for me. I don't know why it was such a shock for me but I really did not expect for him to ask me about coming but it really meant

*Remembrance*

*Earning My Wings*

the world to me. But Tavon was not alone, his mother wanted to attend too. That was the icing on the cake, the two most important people in my life at that time were there for me. They never failed me, nor I them. Tavon searched long and hard to find a scarf to cover the tubing around his neck and at the last minute he found one. I never asked him where did he get it from. When I walked down the aisle with my mom, it was a terrible time for both of us. As we walked down the aisle, we both started crying uncontrollably until we sat down. Tavon and mother came by and shook hands with the family and Tavon shook my mom's hand. When I got back home Tavon told me that when he heard me crying he started to cry too. He told me I felt your pain. At that point, I knew he would always be someone special to me. Not many people feel pain the same way, but knowing he felt mine told me a whole lot about our friendship.

You know it was very hard to deal with the fact that even though Tavon had his own problems to deal with his mom had

*Remembrance*

*Earning My Wings*

some of her own to deal with she had bronchitis something bad and she hated the smell of cigarette smoke it just got to her and choked her up a bit. The family would always try to get mother to go to the hospital and get checked out but you know mother she was not really trying to do all ripping and running back and forth to the doctor's office. She was much too busy working two jobs and trying to make ends meet. Well, we did in fact get mother to go to the hospital and get the necessary treatment that she needed and oddly enough, Tavon was in the hospital too. I was sitting in the hospital room with Tavon and he mentioned mother. I told him that I was up in her room talking to her and I asked him would he like me to call her room so that he could talk to her. He said yes, so I called the operator so she could patch him through to her so that they could talk. It was getting late so while they talked on the phone, I just slide out of the room. I had to catch my bus and go home. After being at work all day I was ready to go. Trust me, I did not want to stay there any longer than I had to aside from helping Tavon if he needed

*Remembrance*

*Earning My Wings*

anything. I came back to mother's room the next day and even though I knew where I stood with them and knew their feelings for me, it still shocked me never the less to have that kind of trust from people that fast! Mother and I talked for a while when I was in Tavon's room. Tavon told me that mother asked where I had been and why I hadn't come to see her in the hospital. She had been waiting for me. That really touched my heart more than I had expressed at that time. It reminded me of when I first came to their house for the first time and Tavon told his mom Leon is going to be here for a long time probably until the day I die. I did not pay that any attention at the time but the truth of the matter it was right on the money. I was there until the day he died. It was as if he already knew that I had no desire to ever leave them like real family and friends are to each other.

It was very hard for me to carry on any kind of close friendship with a patient. The hospital was my place of work and it was an unusual relationship for me to vibe with a patient. The vibes between us was as if we had known each other for years

*Remembrance*

*Earning My Wings*

which caused a lot of dissension between staff members. They had no prior knowledge of us knowing each other before the constant back and fourth, in and out of his room and long conversations. They saw us having made their minds wonder and ask questions to themselves; in turn, they asked questions of Tavon when I was not in the room. Questions about me and my character. What was the relationship between the two of us? Did he mind me being in his room all the time? The nurses thought I should leave him alone and let him get his rest. He understood their plight but his response when they asked him why was I laying across his bed and in his room all day every day was simple. Because I want him to and as long as it does not interfere with my doctor's orders, its alright. So mind your business and do what you are getting paid to do and that is not minding my personal business. I think you want him not to be around me because of your own personal jealous reasons. Well, no he is not going!

It surprised me at how hateful they really were. I had never

*Remembrance*

*Earning My Wings*

encountered this before from the employees at the hospital before. Of course, it spread through the hospital like wild fire about me spending lots of time with a patient on the second floor. It was as if where ever we went there were people watching and asking questions. It seemed as if we were celebrities in the hospital. We enjoyed it to the hilt but you know the beginning of our friendship laying the ground of trust and respect for one another began in the hospital. But no matter were we friends just the same when we walked out in public or even in the hospital people would say are you twins because you look so much alike. Strangers as well as family members would speak about the resemblance it is uncanny. I think that when they say you have a twin out there it must be true because I think I found mine.

On September 18, 1996, that was the last time I would see my dear friend alive. I remember as if it were yesterday. I walked into the room while he lay sleeping and I gave him a slight peck on the cheek. Then he awoke and said, "I was just

*Remembrance*

dreaming about you and now you are here. I was waiting for you."

I did not expect him to be speaking because he hadn't spoken in a few days. He was in so much pain all he could do was grit his teeth. It was a treat for me to hear him talk. He said to me, "you really are a beautiful person and don't let anyone tell you anything less. How long have you been standing there?" I said, "not long, but long enough to see you sleeping. I was just watching you sleep." He laughed. I smiled, it was just so good to see him resting peacefully for once. I was remembering the days before when he wasn't in so much pain; when he wasn't wearing a pamper or having trouble holding his bodily fluids; when he wasn't constantly calling out to go home. "I want to go home, please take me home, I want to go home!" His eyes were sad. I had no control, for once in my life, I had no control It was killing me to see him slipping away slowly, slowly. I leaned over to give him a hug. I remember the smell of his breath, warm and calming to the senses. I had no idea that was the last time I

*Remembrance*

*Earning My Wings*

would see him. I thought to myself that you are my most dearest friend. Even though I had not known you for years, it seemed like centuries and with you nothing else mattered. I swore to you that you would never be forgotten, there is no other friend better than you. I will always love you. Friends like you are really hard to find. I held Tavon's hand and it felt sticky. I asked, "do you want me to wash your hands?" He said, "yes." I soaked a wash cloth in warm water with soap and cleaned his hands and then used some fragranced lotion on his hands. He liked the smell and that meant so much to me because he was so picky, if he did not like something he would just come out and tell you. I had to hurry home even though I did not want leave, but I had to catch my bus and it was pass 11:30 p.m. In a weak whisper he said, "I love you." I said, "know I love you too,"and hurried out the door up the hall. I spoke to the ward clerk for a moment and she told me that he might be getting discharged the next day which was good news. After hearing that I continued to rush to get to the elevator to get downstairs to the bus stop.

*Remembrance*

Thank God, I made it. This all happened on a Wednesday night. I was off work on Thursday, Friday, Saturday, Sunday, but I did not think much about checking in on Tavon. I figured that if he was going home, so I would let him get himself comfortable. Give him a little space. I'd see him either at home or if he had not left the hospital, when I got to work on Monday. This was nothing unusual for us to do so I really thought anything of it until Monday morning.

Tavon's God-brother called and left a message on the answering machine. I did not hear the phone ring, I only saw the light on the machine blinking. I pushed play and heard John say, Marty give me a call. I thought nothing of it so I just fell back to sleep, but 10-15 minutes later either John called back or my roommate Marty heard me when I played the message. I heard Marty open the door and watched as he walked towards me. I was half asleep but awake enough to know what was going on around me. Marty sat in the chair next to my bed and looked over at me with a drained look on his face. It was one of those

*Remembrance*

*Earning My Wings*

"I'm so sorry" looks. At this point, I did not know what was going on. It all happened so fast. He said, "I have something to tell you." I quickly jumped up and out of my bed and stood up and screamed, "No, you don't! You don't have to tell me anything." It was as if I had known all along what was going to be told to me that morning. Marty said, "Leon...Tavon...is gone." I frantically started saying, "NO! That can't be. I have to go and see him." I started getting dressed without even knowing what time it was I went to the bathroom trying to get dressed. I just couldn't do anything right. I forgot how to hold a toothbrush, my hands were shaking so bad I really had a hard time combing my hair, I had Marty call for a cab for me it seemed like it would never come when it did I was beyond ready. I had to see him this was the only thing that I could think of I really could not believe it could be true, no! When I went to the floor that he was on I walked into the room and it was empty clean and neat just like Tavon but there was no Tavon. I didn't know if I'll ever be able to express how I felt at this particular

*Remembrance*

*Earning My Wings*

moment it seemed as if emptiness started to set in and I felt as if I had really lost a part of my heart my dear friend I thought that I could shield you from the ills of the world and assist you in your time of need but I could not shield you nor could I stop the road that you must ravel now and forevermore.

It seemed as if the tragedies were just beginning. It was bad enough that Leon had died with such short notice, but Mother, the base, the ground, the foundation who had held the family together, was on a road of no return. As slippery as that road was it didn't seem like all the brakes in the world could stop the feelings that were building up inside. After learning of Leon's death and making a few phone calls, Mother's asthma started flaring up and when the medics were called they did not give her oxygen quickly enough. The damage was done. She went into cardiac arrest then automatically went into a coma with the lack of oxygen to the brain. After Mother's passing, it was hard for everyone of her remaining children. All we could do is pray. Sometimes our prayers are answered in a way that is truly

*Remembrance*

beneficial for everyone. Other times, even if it is not the way we would like, the prayers are answered just the same. What seems to be the hardest part of all is God's will and man's will are not the same. But, his will is perfect and if we allow him to make the necessary changes in our lives we would be much further than we are. We should not to rely on our own understanding but solely on the understanding of Jesus Christ.

I've heard all those stories of people who have had experiences with ghosts but for some reason things like that didn't bother me. I had no reason to be worried until some things started catching my attention and getting a little out of control. I remember when I came back from Tavon's funeral, I really wanted to go to bed. My body was tired; so much had happened that day, I just about had enough for one day. As I was drifting off to sleep, I started hearing very faint buzzing sounds with this tingling sound like shingling tingles around me. I thought nothing of it at first, it's probably just a mosquito. But the noise started getting louder. My eyes quickly opened and I

*Remembrance*

*Earning My Wings*

said to myself not out loud, you know when you talk to yourself in your head without opening your mouth, WHAT IS THAT! I saw nothing and my windows were closed. I had never had a problem with mosquitos in my room before but I rationalized the sounds by thinking, it's a mosquito. So I put my pillow over my head so that whatever it was would be drowned out and then I could sleep. I remembered that Marty was not there so I couldn't call him in to see if he heard the sounds. So I kept the pillow over my head and went to sleep. The sounds started again. I opened my eyes quickly and the sounds stopped. Again and again it started and then stopped when I opened my eyes. I was surely starting to think that I was going out of my mind. I started thinking that maybe it was Tavon talking to me from in another world. I took a chance and asked the sounds while my eyes were closed if it was Tavon talking to me, even though I was not expecting an answer. The buzzing tingling feeling got extremely loud it scared the living shit out of me I surely was ready to get the hell out of that apartment. I rushed up and went

*Remembrance*

to the bathroom and shut the door quickly. I asked the same question, "Tavon, is that you speaking to me?" I waited a moment or two and then faintly the sounds of shimmering shingles like sparkles over my head began again. I could not believe this, so I called a few friends and told them the story. They told me to open the Bible and read the 23$^{rd}$ Psalm and to leave the Bible open to get rid of evil spirits or anything that is not of God. More than likely, it was not Tavon at all because I know that he would not want to scare me like the way I was scared, so I opened the Bible and read that chapter six or seven times until I could go to sleep. Every night after that was fine. I didn't have any problems after reading the word of God.

A few months had passed and the grieving process was slow but with every day things were getting better and better. One night I dreamed an unexpected dream about Tavon. There were no buzzing or tingling feelings only calmness. I got my chance to see him for the last time. We were in the hospital room where we met and the room was filled with a flourescent white glow.

*Remembrance*

Tavon had on a white gown and he was smiling, and standing strong. He seemed peaceful and happy. Now I rest fine because I know he's in good hands. LOVE YOU STILL!

*Remembrance*

## Resolutions: Inner Peace

I knew I had to find my way to inner peace by finding my own tranquility and the truth. For once in my life I had to be real with myself and once I did, it would be that way from this day forward. Being real would be the hardest thing for me to do and it turned out to be very therapeutic to deal with all the issues that had confronted me within the past few years; the good and the bad. You know, its like learning how to walk again for the very first time. Step by step, sound by sound, until that first step. Come to Mommy. See Daddy, go to Daddy. My, my you sure have grown up. It seems just like yesterday when you were such a happy baby. But you're not a baby anymore. It's graduation day and you have your whole life ahead of you. My, my, you sure have grown up and I am so proud of you.

As the years passed and you have grown and matured into a young adult, I am sure there were times when you felt like facing your problems. However, coming face to face with your

*Resolutions*

problems was nothing short of looking through smoky glass windows. I could hardly see my face in the window. My reflection was very distorted by all the smoke. My eyes couldn't see behind the smoky glass but there was someone who could see right through to my heart. Nothing could be hidden from him, even though I felt most comfortable hiding from life and from God's divine plan for me. Avoiding the truth about the direction of where my life should go could only drive me down a path of complete destruction. I knew that the way in which I was living could not last for long. When you blanket your lies and cloak your hidden agendas so long, it becomes a tug of war with true feelings. It's amazing how mankind's personal chronological approaches to how human kind should and should not be is astounding to me. Let he who is without sin caste the first stone.

I found it most disturbing that whenever I tried to make moves to get into a better situation in my life, there was always someone, somewhere, who tried to dissuade me. They made

*Resolutions*

*Earning My Wings*

their presence known by saying that the things I dreamed of doing weren't what I really wanted. I would just be better off to just leave it alone thus keeping me confused. They would say you will never be anything more than what you are at this moment. What a hurtful thing to say to someone. I was beside myself. I didn't know which way to turn. The furthest thing from my mind was to pray. Why pray? Everything will work out. I knew instinctively what the problem was but I just wasn't ready to face up to the truth about me. I was caught up in living such a worldly life and loving it; that for me the only way I could escape was either to run away, to commit suicide or to allow myself to be put in situations where something bad could happen to me. It seems as if I left the door open for the Devil and it wouldn't be an easy escape for me.

I couldn't do it. Commit suicide? No! My God was not having that. I remember at an early age, about eight or nine years old, I was rummaging through my grandfather's top dresser drawer. I would always go through his things; usually

*Resolutions*

*Earning My Wings*

finding something interesting. To my amazement, this day, I found a handgun. Well, I'd never seen one of those before, you know in person. I had only seen them on the TV box in Westerns. Shoot 'em up Westerns is what my Grandfather would call them. I picked the gun up and I was surprised at how heavy it felt in my small hands. It sure was pretty, all silver and shiny too. I wanted to play Cowboys and Indians. This time, I would be the one with the gun. Little did I know, the Westerns on TV were not real. No one really got hurt in those TV shows, but this gun in my hand could really kill me. For some reason, I knew something wasn't right. I just didn't know exactly what it was, but I just felt it in my gut. Maybe it was all those butterflies flying around in my stomach. Instinctively, I knew this gun wasn't a toy, because I knew toys and this was no toy. It seems as if as soon as I took the gun out of the dresser drawer, I heard little faint voices in my head saying come on, put it to your head. I attempted to do it but I got nervous and my heart seemed to be in my throat. I couldn't even swallow. My nerves were so bad,

*Resolutions*

my mouth got dry. I started to think fast. I didn't know what to do, so I just quickly put the gun back where I found it and I hurried out of Grand Pop's room. I didn't want to get caught in a position I could not explain. Sometimes I would peek into his room but I never got too close to that gun in the top dresser drawer.

I always knew that someone was looking over me at that time in my life. I did not know who or what it was, but soon I found out who he was. His name was Jesus and he was there all the time mindful of the dilemma I had found myself. With me not knowing which way was up, he told me to do the right thing. I had to just listen for the first time in my life and my life would be spared. I had to want to live long enough to see what God had in store for me. I have learned that through prayer all things are possible. And if you only ask the Lord to come into your heart he will. It has been a struggle for me to come to grips with my relationship with the Lord because I know we all fall short of the grace of the Lord. But day by day, I grow closer to the Lord

*Resolutions*

*Earning My Wings*

and my relationship gets stronger and stronger. Yes, I found my way through to inner peace. It's through Jesus!

*Resolutions*

# ABOUT THE AUTHOR

**Leon Franklin Bean III**

I was born March 22, 1973, in Baltimore, Maryland at Lutheran Memorial Hospital to a single mother. My mother and stepfather raised me in a middle class neighborhood. From the very beginning, I had a flair for the creative and I always possessed great sensitivity for people. Growing up as a child and going into my later years as a young adult, I enjoyed performing for people and using all my creativity. In doing this it has allowed me to meet creative people whose lives affect and encourage my writing which helps me to choose the paths that I will go through as far as my writing is concerned. This book has truly bee a labor of love and I do mean labor, because of the trials and tribulations of my life. This book is for not only me; it's for you the reader. I hope you find some comfort in my story.

CPSIA information can be obtained
at www.ICGtesting.com
Printed in the USA
JSHW082326110623
42981JS00001B/37

9 780759 631571